The Power of Student Voices: Influencing Education Policy

Robin Jakai

Copyright © [2023]

Title: The Power of Student Voices: Influencing Education Policy
Author's: Robin Jakai

All rights reserved. No part of this publication may be reproduced, stored in a retrieval system, or transmitted in any form or by any means, electronic, mechanical, photocopying, recording, or otherwise, without the prior written permission of the publisher or author, except in the case of brief quotations embodied in critical reviews and certain other non-commercial uses permitted by copyright law.

This book was printed and published by [Publisher's: **Robin Jakai**] in [2023]

ISBN:

TABLE OF CONTENT

Chapter 1: Understanding Education Policy 06

The Importance of Education Policy

How Education Policy Impacts Students

The Role of Student Voices in Shaping Education Policy

Chapter 2: Advocating for Change 13

The Power of Student Activism

Building a Strong Student Voice Movement

Strategies for Effectively Communicating with Policy Makers

Chapter 3: Student-Led Initiatives 20

Creating Student-Led Organizations

Successful Examples of Student-Led Initiatives

Overcoming Challenges in Implementing Student-Led Initiatives

Chapter 4: Collaborating with Education Stakeholders 27

Engaging Teachers and Educators in Policy Discussions

Partnering with Parents and Parent Organizations

The Role of Community Leaders in Education Policy

Chapter 5: The Impact of Student Voices 33

Case Studies: How Student Voices Have Influenced Education Policy

Evaluating the Effectiveness of Student Advocacy

Measuring the Long-Term Impact of Student Voices on Education Policy

Chapter 6: Empowering Student Voices 39

Providing Resources and Support for Student Advocacy

Encouraging Student Leadership in Schools and Communities

Fostering a Culture of Active Citizenship among Students

Chapter 1: Understanding Education Policy

The Importance of Education Policy

Education policy plays a crucial role in shaping the future of our educational system. It is an essential aspect of public policy that directly impacts students like you. In this subchapter, we will explore the significance of education policy and how your voice can influence its development.

Education policy refers to the set of rules, regulations, and guidelines that govern educational institutions and practices. It encompasses various areas, including curriculum development, assessment methods, teacher training, funding allocation, and educational access. These policies are formulated by policymakers who aim to improve the quality of education and ensure equal opportunities for all students.

One of the primary reasons why education policy is crucial is its potential to create a fair and inclusive learning environment. Policies can address educational disparities among different socioeconomic backgrounds and ensure that every student has access to quality education. By advocating for equitable policies, you can contribute to creating a level playing field for all students, irrespective of their background or circumstances.

Education policy also determines the content and structure of your curriculum. It influences what you learn, how it is taught, and the methods used for assessment. By actively participating in discussions and providing your input, you can influence the development of a curriculum that is relevant, engaging, and prepares you for the challenges of the future.

Furthermore, education policy plays a vital role in the professional development of teachers. Policies can shape the training programs, mentoring initiatives, and support systems available to educators. By voicing your opinions on teacher training and development, you can contribute to creating a supportive environment that enhances the effectiveness of teachers and, consequently, improves your learning experience.

Additionally, education policy determines the allocation of resources to educational institutions. Adequate funding is essential for providing necessary infrastructure, learning materials, and extracurricular activities. By advocating for increased funding and fair distribution, you can help ensure that your school has all the necessary resources to foster a conducive learning environment.

Your voice as a student is crucial in shaping education policy. By actively engaging in discussions, participating in student organizations, and communicating your thoughts to policymakers, you can influence the development and implementation of policies that directly impact your education. Your experiences, challenges, and ideas are invaluable in creating a student-centered educational system.

In conclusion, education policy plays a vital role in shaping the future of education. It determines the quality of education, equal opportunities for all students, curriculum content, teacher training, and resource allocation. As students, your voice is powerful and can influence these policies. By actively participating in discussions and advocating for equitable and student-centered policies, you can contribute to creating an inclusive and effective education system that prepares you for a successful future.

How Education Policy Impacts Students

Chapter 4: How Education Policy Impacts Students

Education policy plays a crucial role in shaping the educational landscape for students. From curriculum design to funding allocation, policy decisions directly affect students' learning experiences, opportunities, and future prospects. In this subchapter, we will explore the various ways education policy impacts students and why it is vital for students to understand and engage with policy-making processes.

1. Quality of Education: Education policies determine the standards and expectations for schools and teachers. These policies directly influence the quality of education students receive. By advocating for policies that prioritize rigorous academic standards, personalized learning, and innovative teaching methods, students can ensure they receive a high-quality education that prepares them for success.

2. Access to Resources: Education policies also determine the allocation of resources such as textbooks, technology, and extracurricular activities. Students who actively engage in education policy discussions can advocate for equitable distribution of resources, ensuring that all students have access to the tools and opportunities necessary for their academic and personal growth.

3. School Climate and Safety: Education policy plays a significant role in shaping the school climate and ensuring students' safety. Policies addressing issues such as bullying prevention, mental health support, and disciplinary practices have a direct impact on students' well-being. By participating in policy discussions, students can influence the creation of safe and inclusive learning environments.

4. College and Career Readiness: Education policies also shape the pathways to higher education and career readiness. Policies related to college admissions, financial aid, and career and technical education impact students' ability to pursue their desired careers. By engaging in policy advocacy, students can ensure that these pathways are accessible and equitable for all.

5. Civic Engagement and Democracy: Education policy provides opportunities for students to develop civic engagement skills and become active participants in democracy. Policies that promote civic education, student voice, and community involvement empower students to be informed citizens who can contribute meaningfully to society.

Understanding how education policy impacts students empowers them to advocate for their rights and ensure their voices are heard. By actively engaging in policy discussions, students can shape the education system to better meet their needs and aspirations. Together, students have the power to influence education policy and create a more equitable and inclusive educational landscape for themselves and future generations.

The Role of Student Voices in Shaping Education Policy

Introduction

In today's rapidly changing world, the voice of students is becoming increasingly important in shaping education policy. This subchapter explores the power of student voices and their significant role in influencing education policies. Students, as the primary beneficiaries of the education system, possess unique insights, experiences, and perspectives that can greatly contribute to the improvement of educational policies.

Empowering Students as Change Agents
Students are not only the recipients of education but also active participants in the learning process. By empowering students and encouraging them to share their perspectives, we can create a more inclusive and effective education system. When students are given a platform to voice their opinions, they become change agents who can influence policies to better meet their needs.

Understanding Student Needs
No one understands the challenges and needs of students better than the students themselves. By actively involving students in policy discussions, policymakers gain valuable insights into the issues they face on a daily basis. Whether it's addressing the lack of resources, improving mental health support, or promoting inclusivity, students' voices provide crucial guidance for policymakers.

Promoting Student Well-being
Education policy should prioritize the well-being of students, and who better to provide input on this than the students themselves? By

actively seeking student perspectives, policymakers can identify areas where improvements are needed, such as reducing stress levels, enhancing school safety, or fostering a positive learning environment. Student voices can bring attention to these important issues and drive policy changes that prioritize student well-being.

Fostering Civic Engagement

Engaging students in the policymaking process not only benefits education policy but also develops their understanding of democratic principles and civic responsibility. By actively participating in discussions and decision-making, students learn about the importance of being informed, engaged citizens. This involvement not only shapes policies but also empowers students to become active participants in shaping their own future.

Conclusion

The power of student voices in influencing education policy cannot be underestimated. By recognizing the unique perspectives and needs of students, policymakers can make well-informed decisions that have a positive impact on the education system as a whole. Engaging students in policy discussions fosters a sense of ownership and empowerment, transforming them into active agents of change. Students, as the ultimate beneficiaries of education, deserve to have their voices heard and play a vital role in shaping the policies that govern their own learning journeys.

Chapter 2: Advocating for Change

The Power of Student Activism

In today's rapidly changing world, student activism has emerged as a powerful force that is shaping and influencing education policy like never before. Students, as the primary stakeholders in the education system, possess a unique perspective and firsthand experience that can drive meaningful change. This subchapter explores the transformative power of student activism and highlights its profound impact on public policy.

Student activism is a platform that enables students to raise their voices and advocate for their rights, interests, and concerns. It empowers them to challenge the status quo, question established norms, and demand accountability from policymakers. By organizing protests, demonstrations, and awareness campaigns, students can bring attention to pressing issues and initiate dialogues that lead to tangible policy changes.

One of the most notable examples of student activism's impact on public policy can be seen in the realm of education funding. Throughout history, students have played a pivotal role in advocating for increased investment in education. By mobilizing their peers, engaging with legislators, and raising public awareness, students have successfully influenced policymakers to allocate more resources to schools and universities, ensuring access to quality education for all.

Moreover, student activism has also proven instrumental in promoting inclusivity and diversity within educational institutions.

Students have been at the forefront of movements advocating for equal opportunities, challenging discriminatory practices, and demanding curriculum reforms that reflect the experiences and histories of marginalized communities. By amplifying their voices, students have pushed policymakers to adopt policies that foster an inclusive and equitable learning environment.

Furthermore, student activism extends beyond local boundaries, as students now have access to global platforms through social media and online networks. This interconnectedness has allowed student activists to collaborate and share ideas across borders, leading to a global movement for change. From climate change activism to advocating for mental health resources, students are mobilizing like never before to address the pressing challenges of our time.

In conclusion, student activism is a powerful tool that allows students to influence public policy and shape the future of education. By harnessing their collective voices, students have the ability to challenge existing norms, demand accountability, and effect positive change. As students, you have the power to make a difference and create an educational system that represents your interests and values. Embrace the power of student activism and join the movement for a better education system. Your voice matters, and together, we can shape the policies that will shape our future.

Building a Strong Student Voice Movement

In recent years, students have been increasingly recognized as powerful agents of change in the educational landscape. Their unique perspectives, experiences, and insights have the potential to shape and influence education policy in profound ways. This subchapter aims to empower students by providing guidance on how to build a strong student voice movement and effectively advocate for educational policy changes.

1. Unleashing the Power of Student Voices

The first step in building a strong student voice movement is recognizing the value of your voice. Understand that your experiences and opinions matter and can contribute to creating positive change in education. Embrace your role as a catalyst for improvement.

2. Forming Alliances and Collaborations

To amplify your impact, it is crucial to form alliances and collaborate with like-minded individuals and organizations. Seek out student organizations, advocacy groups, and educators who are passionate about education policy. By working together, you can pool resources, share knowledge, and build a stronger movement.

3. Building a Cohesive Narrative

Developing a cohesive narrative is essential in gaining public support for your cause. Craft a clear and compelling message that highlights the issues you want to address and the positive outcomes you envision. Tell your stories, share your experiences, and make the case for change in a way that resonates with policymakers, educators, and the wider community.

4. Utilizing Technology and Social Media

Harness the power of technology and social media to mobilize and engage a larger audience. Utilize platforms such as Twitter, Facebook, and Instagram to share information, raise awareness, and organize campaigns. Leverage the online space to connect with other student advocates, share resources, and inspire action.

5. Engaging with Policymakers

Engaging with policymakers is crucial to ensure that student voices are heard at the highest levels. Attend public meetings, forums, and legislative sessions to express your concerns and propose solutions. Write letters, make phone calls, and use social media to directly communicate with decision-makers. Remember, your opinions carry weight, and policymakers need to understand the impact of educational policies on students directly from those they affect.

6. Sustaining the Movement

Building a strong student voice movement is an ongoing process. It requires dedication, perseverance, and adaptability. Develop strategies to sustain the movement, such as leadership succession plans, mentorship programs, and regular communication channels. Nurture a culture of student advocacy that transcends individual graduating classes and creates a lasting impact.

By building a strong student voice movement, you can play a pivotal role in shaping education policies that truly reflect the needs and aspirations of students. Your voices have the power to influence and transform the educational landscape, paving the way for a brighter future. Embrace the opportunity, collaborate with others, and let your collective voices be heard. Together, we can create an education system that empowers and supports every student.

Strategies for Effectively Communicating with Policy Makers

When it comes to influencing education policy, one of the most powerful tools at your disposal is your voice. As students, you have a unique perspective and firsthand experience of the challenges and opportunities within the education system. By effectively communicating with policy makers, you can directly influence the decisions that will shape your educational journey and that of future generations. Here are some strategies to help you make your voice heard:

1. Research and understand the policy landscape: Before engaging with policy makers, it is crucial to have a solid understanding of the current policies and initiatives in place. Educate yourself about the issues that matter to you and the potential solutions being discussed. This will enable you to speak confidently and knowledgeably when advocating for change.

2. Develop a clear message: To effectively communicate with policy makers, it is essential to have a clear and concise message. Identify the key points you want to convey and articulate them in a way that is easy to understand. Consider the impact your proposed changes will have on students, teachers, and the overall education system. Craft a compelling narrative that resonates with policy makers' goals and priorities.

3. Build relationships and coalitions: Policy makers are more likely to listen to students when they see a united front. Collaborate with fellow students, teachers, and community members who share your concerns. Form coalitions and organizations that amplify your

message and demonstrate broad support. Building relationships with policy makers and their staff can also be beneficial in establishing trust and understanding.

4. Utilize multiple communication channels: Policy makers receive numerous requests and messages daily. To stand out, employ a variety of communication channels. Write personalized letters or emails, make phone calls, and consider organizing meetings or attending public hearings. Utilize social media platforms to raise awareness and engage in conversations with policy makers and their constituents.

5. Be persistent and follow up: Policy making is a complex and often slow process. It is important to be persistent and follow up on your communications. If you don't receive a response, don't be discouraged. Reach out again, emphasizing the importance of your message. Stay engaged and continue advocating for change, even if progress is not immediate.

6. Be respectful and professional: When communicating with policy makers, always maintain a respectful and professional tone. Avoid personal attacks or inflammatory language. Instead, focus on the issues and present your arguments with evidence and logical reasoning. Remember, policy makers are more likely to listen to well-informed and respectful voices.

By employing these strategies, you can effectively communicate with policy makers and influence education policy. Your voice has the power to shape the future of education and ensure that it meets the needs of students. Embrace the responsibility and seize the opportunity to make a lasting impact on public policy.

Chapter 3: Student-Led Initiatives

Creating Student-Led Organizations

In today's rapidly changing world, students have an increasingly important role to play in shaping education policy. Student voices are powerful and have the potential to influence decision-making processes that directly impact their lives. One effective way for students to make their voices heard is through the creation of student-led organizations. These organizations provide a platform for students to come together, collaborate, and advocate for positive change in the realm of public policy.

Student-led organizations offer numerous benefits to those who participate. By taking an active role in a student-led organization, students can develop leadership skills, learn about the intricacies of public policy, and gain valuable experience in grassroots advocacy. These organizations also provide an avenue for students to connect with like-minded individuals who share their passion for education policy. Through collaboration, students can leverage their collective voice to advocate for policies that address their needs and concerns.

When creating a student-led organization, it is important to start with a clear vision and mission. Define the purpose of the organization and identify the specific goals and objectives you hope to achieve. This will serve as a guiding framework for your organization's activities and initiatives. Additionally, it is vital to establish a strong leadership structure within the organization. Identify individuals who are passionate about the cause and have the necessary skills to effectively lead and manage the organization. Delegation, teamwork, and effective communication are key to ensuring the success of any student-led organization.

Once your organization is established, it is essential to build connections and collaborate with other stakeholders, such as school administrators, policymakers, and community leaders. By engaging in open and constructive dialogue, you can cultivate relationships that will allow for meaningful discussions on education policy. These connections can be instrumental in pushing for policy changes that align with the needs and aspirations of students.

Remember, student-led organizations are only as strong as the individuals involved. Encourage active participation and create an inclusive environment where every student feels valued and heard. Take advantage of social media platforms and other digital tools to amplify your message and reach a wider audience. By harnessing the power of technology, you can mobilize students from across the country to join your cause and effect change on a broader scale.

Creating student-led organizations is a powerful way for students to influence education policy. By coming together, organizing, and advocating for their rights and needs, students can shape the future of education. Your voice matters, and by taking action, you can make a difference in the policies that govern your education. Step up, create a student-led organization, and be the change you want to see in the world of public policy.

Successful Examples of Student-Led Initiatives

In recent years, students have been at the forefront of driving meaningful change in education policy. Their voices, ideas, and initiatives have proven to be powerful catalysts in shaping the future of education. In this subchapter, we will explore some inspiring examples of successful student-led initiatives that have made a significant impact on public policy.

One remarkable example is the Students for Educational Reform (SER) movement. SER originated from a group of passionate high school students who recognized the need for comprehensive reform in their underprivileged community. These students tirelessly advocated for increased funding, improved resources, and enhanced teacher training. Through their persuasive efforts, they successfully influenced local legislators to allocate additional funds to their schools, resulting in improved educational opportunities for thousands of students.

Another notable initiative is the Youth Climate Strike movement, initiated by Greta Thunberg, a Swedish student turned global climate activist. Greta's solo strike outside the Swedish Parliament inspired millions of students worldwide to join her cause. Students from different corners of the world united, demanding immediate action against climate change. Their collective voice led to policy changes, with governments enacting stricter climate regulations and committing to renewable energy sources. The Youth Climate Strike movement serves as a powerful reminder that students hold the potential to shape policies that impact their future.

Furthermore, the recent Black Lives Matter (BLM) movement witnessed a remarkable surge of student-led initiatives. Students organized protests, educational campaigns, and policy advocacy to address systemic racism in education. Their efforts led to the implementation of diversity and inclusion programs in schools, reforming curriculum to include more inclusive history, and increased funding for schools serving marginalized communities. The BLM movement exemplifies the power of student voices in pushing for equity and justice within the education system.

These examples highlight the immense potential of student-led initiatives in influencing education policy. It is crucial for students to recognize their collective power and harness it to create meaningful change. By organizing themselves, speaking out, and engaging with policymakers, students can shape policies that address the challenges they face in their education.

To empower student voices further, this book provides practical advice, strategies, and case studies to guide students in building effective initiatives. It emphasizes the importance of collaboration, research, and persistence in influencing education policy. By learning from successful examples and leveraging their own experiences, students can become powerful advocates for educational equity and quality.

As students, your voices matter. You have the power to shape the policies that will determine the future of education. Through the examples shared in this subchapter, we hope to inspire you to take action, collaborate with your peers, and make a difference in the realm of public policy. Together, let's harness the power of student voices and create a brighter future for education.

Overcoming Challenges in Implementing Student-Led Initiatives

Introduction:
Implementing student-led initiatives in the realm of public policy can be a powerful tool for influencing education policy. By actively engaging in the decision-making processes that shape their own learning experiences, students can drive meaningful change and have their voices heard. However, such endeavors are not without their challenges. In this subchapter, we will explore some of the hurdles that students may encounter when trying to implement student-led initiatives and strategies for overcoming them.

1. Lack of Support:
One of the primary challenges faced by students is the lack of support from key stakeholders such as school administrators, policymakers, and even fellow students. To overcome this, it is crucial to build strong alliances and coalitions. Forming partnerships with like-minded individuals and organizations, showcasing the benefits of student-led initiatives, and presenting well-researched proposals can help garner support and increase the likelihood of success.

2. Resistance to Change:
Institutional resistance to change is another obstacle that students may encounter. Many educational institutions are resistant to deviating from traditional approaches and structures. To overcome this challenge, it is important to present compelling arguments supported by data and research to demonstrate the effectiveness and benefits of student-led initiatives. Engaging in dialogue with decision-makers and showcasing successful case studies can help alleviate concerns and foster a culture of openness to change.

3.   Limited   Resources:
Implementing student-led initiatives requires resources, including time, funding, and access to information. Students often face challenges in securing these resources. To overcome this hurdle, students can tap into existing networks and organizations that support student activism. Additionally, crowdfunding, seeking grants, and leveraging social media platforms can help raise funds and amplify their message.

4.   Sustaining   Momentum:
Maintaining momentum and sustaining interest in student-led initiatives can be a challenge, as students have multiple responsibilities and commitments. To address this, it is essential to establish clear goals, create a structured framework, and delegate responsibilities among team members. Regular communication, evaluation, and celebration of milestones can help maintain enthusiasm and ensure the longevity of the initiative.

Conclusion:

Implementing student-led initiatives in the realm of public policy can be a transformative experience for students, enabling them to influence education policy and shape their own learning environments. While challenges may arise, overcoming them is possible through building alliances, presenting compelling arguments, securing resources, and sustaining momentum. By empowering students to overcome these challenges, we can unleash the true power of student voices in shaping the future of education policy.

Chapter 4: Collaborating with Education Stakeholders

Engaging Teachers and Educators in Policy Discussions

In the realm of public policy, the voices of students are an invaluable asset when it comes to influencing education policies. However, it is equally important to recognize the significant role that teachers and educators play in shaping these policies. After all, these are the individuals who interact with students on a daily basis, understand their needs, and witness the impact of policies firsthand. Engaging teachers and educators in policy discussions is crucial to ensure that the education system meets the diverse needs of students.

Teachers and educators possess a wealth of knowledge and experience that can contribute to the development of effective policies. Their insights and expertise can shed light on the practical aspects of education, including teaching methods, curriculum design, and classroom management. By involving them in policy discussions, we can tap into their valuable perspectives and ensure that policies are grounded in the realities of the classroom.

In addition, engaging teachers and educators in policy discussions fosters a sense of ownership and empowerment. When they are given the opportunity to contribute to policy-making, they feel valued and recognized for their dedication and expertise. This, in turn, enhances their motivation and commitment to their profession. By involving teachers and educators, policy discussions become more inclusive and democratic, allowing for a wider range of perspectives to be considered.

Furthermore, teachers and educators are key stakeholders in the education system. They have a deep understanding of the challenges and opportunities that students face, and are well-positioned to advocate for their needs. By actively involving them in policy discussions, we can ensure that policies are responsive to the unique circumstances of different communities and student populations.

To effectively engage teachers and educators in policy discussions, it is essential to establish open channels of communication and create platforms for their input. This can be done through regular meetings, workshops, or online forums where they can share their ideas and concerns. Additionally, policymakers should actively seek their feedback and involve them in the decision-making process.

In conclusion, engaging teachers and educators in policy discussions is crucial for creating an education system that truly meets the needs of students. By tapping into their expertise, involving them in decision-making processes, and valuing their contributions, we can develop policies that are grounded in the realities of the classroom and inclusive of diverse perspectives. It is through this collaborative approach that we can harness the power of student voices and shape a brighter future for education.

Partnering with Parents and Parent Organizations

As students, we have a unique perspective on education policy and its impact on our lives. Our voices matter, and we can play a significant role in influencing the decisions made at the policy level. However, we shouldn't underestimate the power of partnering with parents and parent organizations to amplify our message and create meaningful change.

Parents are our biggest advocates. They share our desire for quality education and are often more experienced in navigating the intricacies of policy-making. By partnering with them, we can tap into their knowledge and learn from their experiences. They can guide us on the most effective ways to engage with policymakers, connect us with influential individuals, and provide valuable insights into the policy landscape.

Parent organizations, such as Parent-Teacher Associations (PTAs) or Parent-Teacher-Student Associations (PTSAs), are excellent platforms for collaboration. These organizations are dedicated to promoting the welfare of students and their families. By joining or collaborating with them, we can leverage their networks, resources, and expertise to advocate for policies that benefit all students.

One way to partner with parents and parent organizations is by organizing joint advocacy campaigns. By aligning our goals and working together, we can amplify our voice and increase our chances of success. We can create petitions, organize rallies, and attend public hearings as a united front, sending a powerful message to policymakers that we are serious about our demands.

Additionally, parents are often more connected to local and national policymakers than we are. They attend school board meetings, participate in community events, and build relationships with elected officials. By engaging with parents, we can tap into these networks and gain access to decision-makers who can shape education policy. We can invite them to student-led forums or invite them to join our advocacy efforts, forging mutually beneficial partnerships.

Moreover, parents can provide valuable perspectives and insights that policymakers may overlook. They can share personal stories, experiences, and concerns that highlight the real-life impact of policies on students and families. By including their narratives in our advocacy efforts, we can make our message more compelling and relatable, increasing the chances of policy change.

In conclusion, partnering with parents and parent organizations is crucial for students engaged in public policy advocacy. By collaborating with them, we can tap into their knowledge, networks, and experiences to amplify our voices and create meaningful change. Together, we can work towards policies that ensure a high-quality education for all students.

The Role of Community Leaders in Education Policy

As students, we often find ourselves at the receiving end of education policies and reforms that affect our daily lives. It's easy to feel like our voices are not heard or that we have no control over the decisions made by policymakers. However, it is important to recognize the significant role that community leaders play in shaping education policy and advocating for student needs.

Community leaders are individuals who possess both a deep understanding of the local education system and a genuine concern for the welfare of students. They can be parents, teachers, principals, school board members, or even students themselves. These leaders have the power to influence education policy at various levels, from the local to the national level.

One of the primary roles of community leaders in education policy is to act as advocates for students. They work tirelessly to ensure that the voices and concerns of students are heard by policymakers. By engaging in dialogue with students, conducting surveys, and organizing meetings, community leaders gather valuable insights into the challenges faced by students and use this information to inform policy decisions.

Additionally, community leaders also have the responsibility to bridge the gap between policymakers and students. They act as intermediaries, conveying student perspectives to policymakers and helping policymakers understand the real-life implications of their decisions. By acting as a liaison, community leaders facilitate meaningful discussions between all stakeholders involved in education policy-making, leading to more student-centric policies.

Furthermore, community leaders are instrumental in mobilizing resources to support education initiatives. They collaborate with local businesses, non-profit organizations, and government agencies to secure funding and resources for schools. By leveraging their connections and influence, community leaders ensure that students have access to quality education, extracurricular activities, and support services.

To maximize the impact of community leaders, students must actively engage with them and voice their concerns. By participating in school board meetings, joining student councils, or organizing grassroots campaigns, students can collaborate with community leaders to effect change. It is crucial for students to understand that their opinions matter and that they have the power to shape education policy.

In conclusion, community leaders play a vital role in education policy by advocating for students, bridging the gap between policymakers and students, and mobilizing resources. As students, we must recognize the impact that community leaders have on our education system and actively engage with them to ensure our voices are heard. By working together, we can create a more inclusive and student-centric education system that meets the needs of all.

Chapter 5: The Impact of Student Voices

Case Studies: How Student Voices Have Influenced Education Policy

In recent years, the power of student voices in shaping education policy has gained significant attention. Students, like you, have the potential to influence decisions that directly impact your education and the education of future generations. This subchapter aims to provide you with inspiring case studies that demonstrate the remarkable impact student voices can have on shaping education policy.

One remarkable case study comes from a group of high school students in a small town who were passionate about improving mental health support in their schools. Recognizing the lack of access to mental health resources and the negative impact it had on their peers, these students took it upon themselves to advocate for change. They organized town hall meetings, conducted surveys, and even met with local policymakers to share their stories and concerns. Their efforts paid off when the school district responded by implementing a comprehensive mental health program, providing support to students in need and prioritizing mental wellness.

Another inspiring case study involves college students who were concerned about the rising cost of textbooks. They recognized that expensive textbooks were hindering their access to quality education. Students formed a coalition, conducted research, and collaborated with professors and administrators to find viable solutions. Through their advocacy and perseverance, they successfully influenced the university to implement affordable textbook initiatives, such as open educational resources and textbook rental programs. As a result, students were able to save thousands of dollars on textbooks, making education more accessible and affordable for all.

Furthermore, student voices have also played a significant role in shaping public policy at the national level. For instance, a group of students concerned about climate change organized a nationwide movement, demanding action from policymakers. Their relentless activism, including strikes, rallies, and social media campaigns, pushed climate change to the top of the political agenda. As a result, governments around the world began implementing policies to reduce carbon emissions and invest in renewable energy sources.

These case studies highlight the power of student voices in influencing education policy. They demonstrate that students, regardless of their age or educational level, have the ability to effect meaningful change. By sharing your stories, concerns, and ideas, you can shape the future of education in your community, your country, and even the world.

In conclusion, this subchapter serves as a reminder that your voice matters. It showcases the potential impact that student voices have on education policy and encourages you to be an active participant in shaping your own educational experience. By standing up, speaking out, and working together, you can bring about positive change and create a better future for all students.

Evaluating the Effectiveness of Student Advocacy

In the realm of public policy, student advocacy plays a crucial role in shaping education policies that directly affect students' lives. The power of student voices cannot be underestimated, as their perspectives and experiences offer unique insights and drive positive change. This subchapter aims to explore the importance of evaluating the effectiveness of student advocacy, highlighting the impact it can have on education policy.

First and foremost, evaluating the effectiveness of student advocacy provides a means to measure the success and impact of their efforts. By assessing the outcomes of their initiatives, students can determine whether their advocacy strategies and messages are resonating with policymakers and influencing policy decisions. This evaluation process helps students identify areas of strength and areas for improvement, allowing them to refine their approaches and increase their effectiveness over time.

Furthermore, evaluating student advocacy efforts allows students to gather evidence that can be used to demonstrate the importance of their voices in shaping education policy. By collecting data, statistics, and personal stories of the impact of certain policies, students can present a compelling case to policymakers, making it harder to ignore their perspectives. This evidence-based approach strengthens the credibility and legitimacy of student advocacy, increasing the chances of policy changes aligning with students' needs and aspirations.

Additionally, evaluating the effectiveness of student advocacy promotes accountability among policymakers. By monitoring the progress and outcomes of advocacy initiatives, students can hold policymakers accountable for the promises they have made or the commitments they have failed to uphold. This accountability fosters a sense of responsibility among policymakers and encourages them to take student perspectives seriously when making decisions that directly affect education policies.

Lastly, evaluating student advocacy helps build a strong foundation for future advocacy efforts. By documenting and sharing successful strategies, students can pass on valuable knowledge and lessons learned to future generations of advocates. This creates a cycle of continuous improvement, where each wave of student advocates can learn from those who came before them and build upon their successes.

In conclusion, evaluating the effectiveness of student advocacy is a crucial step in the process of influencing education policy. It allows students to measure their impact, gather evidence, hold policymakers accountable, and build a solid foundation for future advocacy efforts. By recognizing the power of their voices and engaging in rigorous evaluation, students can truly make a difference in shaping the policies that shape their education and future.

Measuring the Long-Term Impact of Student Voices on Education Policy

One of the most powerful forces for change in education policy is the collective voice of students. As students, you have a unique perspective on the challenges and opportunities within the education system. Your experiences, ideas, and insights can shape policies that directly impact your lives and those of future generations.

But how can we measure the long-term impact of student voices on education policy? How can we ensure that the changes implemented actually lead to meaningful improvements in the quality of education? These are essential questions that both policymakers and students need to consider.

Firstly, it is crucial to recognize that student voices are not a one-time event, but an ongoing process. Your input should not be limited to a single survey or a few public hearings. Instead, your voices should be integrated into the entire policymaking cycle, from agenda-setting to implementation and evaluation. This ensures that your perspectives are continuously considered and that policies are responsive to your evolving needs.

Secondly, measuring the long-term impact requires a comprehensive evaluation framework. This framework should assess both the short-term outcomes and the long-term effects of policies influenced by student voices. Short-term outcomes may include changes in curriculum, teacher-student relationships, or access to resources. However, it is equally important to measure the long-term effects, such as graduation rates, college enrollment, and career success. By analyzing these indicators, policymakers can determine whether the policies influenced by students have had a lasting positive impact on education.

Moreover, students themselves can play an active role in measuring the impact of their voices on policy. By collecting data, conducting surveys, and participating in research, you can contribute to the evidence base that informs policy decisions. This not only strengthens the credibility of your voices but also empowers you as active agents of change.

Lastly, it is essential to recognize that the impact of student voices extends beyond the realm of education. By advocating for changes in education policy, you are also influencing broader public policy agendas. Education is intimately linked to social, economic, and political issues, and your voices can shape policies that address inequality, promote social justice, and create a more inclusive society.

In conclusion, measuring the long-term impact of student voices on education policy requires a comprehensive and continuous approach. By integrating student perspectives throughout the policymaking cycle, evaluating both short-term outcomes and long-term effects, and actively engaging students in data collection and research, we can ensure that your voices lead to meaningful and lasting improvements in education. Together, let us harness the power of student voices to influence public policy and create a brighter future for all.

Chapter 6: Empowering Student Voices

Providing Resources and Support for Student Advocacy

As students, you possess a powerful voice that has the potential to shape and influence education policy in your communities. Your unique perspectives, experiences, and ideas are invaluable assets that can drive positive change. However, advocating for your rights and concerns may seem like an overwhelming task. This subchapter aims to provide you with essential resources and support to help you become effective advocates for education policy reform.

1. Knowledge is Key: To be an effective advocate, it is crucial to stay informed about current education policies and issues. Regularly research and read up on local, state, and national education policies, as well as their potential impact on students like yourself. Websites, blogs, and articles from reliable sources can provide you with the necessary information to articulate your concerns and demands.

2. Establish Student-Led Organizations: Forming student-led organizations is an excellent way to channel your collective voice and advocate for change. These organizations can provide a platform for students to come together, share ideas, and work towards common goals. Collaborate with like-minded individuals and create student unions, clubs, or associations dedicated to advocating for student rights and educational improvements.

3. Engaging with Public Policy: Familiarize yourself with the processes involved in shaping public

policy. Attend local school board meetings, education-related town halls, and public hearings to observe and learn how decisions are made. Additionally, reach out to elected officials, policymakers, and education stakeholders to express your concerns, ideas, and suggestions. Establishing personal connections can help ensure your voice is heard.

4.   Utilize   Social   Media   Platforms: Harness the power of social media to amplify your advocacy efforts. Create accounts on platforms like Twitter, Instagram, or TikTok, and use them to share your experiences, knowledge, and demands. Share stories, create informative graphics, or record short videos to engage a wider audience and raise awareness about the issues you care about.

5.   Seek   Mentorship   and   Collaboration: Connect with individuals and organizations already engaged in education policy advocacy. Seek mentorship from experienced advocates who can guide and support you on your journey. Collaborate with other student advocacy groups or established nonprofits working towards similar goals. By joining forces, you can amplify your collective impact and create lasting change.

Remember, your voice matters, and your advocacy can make a difference. By utilizing these resources and support systems, you can effectively influence education policy, ensuring that the voices of students like you are heard and valued. Together, we can build a better educational system that meets the needs and aspirations of all students.

Encouraging Student Leadership in Schools and Communities

In today's rapidly changing world, the role of student leaders has never been more crucial. As young individuals, students possess unique perspectives, fresh ideas, and the passion needed to make a difference in their schools and communities. This subchapter aims to explore the power of student voices and the ways in which they can influence education policy, ultimately shaping the future of our society.

Student leadership is not limited to holding official positions, such as being a class representative or student council member. It encompasses a much broader scope that involves taking initiative, being proactive, and making positive contributions to one's surroundings. By encouraging student leadership in schools and communities, we can foster a culture of collaboration, innovation, and social responsibility among students.

One of the key benefits of student leadership is the opportunity for personal growth and development. By taking on leadership roles, students learn valuable skills such as effective communication, critical thinking, problem-solving, and teamwork. These skills are not only essential for their academic success but also for their future careers and life beyond the classroom.

Furthermore, student leaders have the unique ability to influence education policy. By voicing their opinions and concerns, students can contribute to the decision-making processes that shape their educational experiences. They can provide insights into the effectiveness of teaching methods, curriculum design, and school policies, ultimately leading to improvements in the overall education system.

In order to encourage student leadership, schools and communities must create an environment that values and supports student initiatives. This can be achieved by establishing platforms for student voices to be heard, such as student-led forums, advisory boards, or mentorship programs. Additionally, providing training and resources for student leaders can further enhance their skills and empower them to take on greater responsibilities.

Public policy plays a crucial role in shaping the educational landscape. By actively participating in public policy discussions and advocating for their rights and needs, students can influence policy decisions that directly impact their educational experiences. Through collaborative efforts with policymakers, students can drive positive changes in areas such as equitable access to education, student mental health support, and inclusive curriculum.

In conclusion, encouraging student leadership in schools and communities is vital for the holistic development of students and the betterment of society. By empowering student voices and involving them in decision-making processes, we can create an education system that truly meets the needs and aspirations of its learners. Students have the power to shape the policies that shape their educational journeys, and it is essential for them to recognize and embrace this potential. Let your voices be heard and make a lasting impact on education policy and the world around you.

Fostering a Culture of Active Citizenship among Students

As students, you have a powerful voice that can shape the future of education policy. The ability to understand and actively engage in public policy is crucial to ensuring that your needs and concerns are heard and addressed. This subchapter aims to inspire and guide you in fostering a culture of active citizenship, empowering you to become agents of change in the field of education policy.

Active citizenship begins with awareness and education. Start by familiarizing yourself with the policy-making process and understanding how decisions are made. This knowledge will enable you to effectively advocate for the changes you want to see. Stay informed about current policies, debates, and initiatives in education. Engage in dialogues with your peers, teachers, and even policymakers to gain different perspectives and expand your understanding.

Once you are well-informed, it is time to take action. Start by joining or forming student organizations focused on education policy. These groups provide a platform to collaborate with like-minded individuals, share ideas, and amplify your collective voice. Together, you can identify key issues, develop strategies, and propose innovative solutions to address them.

Another effective way to foster active citizenship is through community engagement. Organize events, workshops, or forums to raise awareness about education policy among your fellow students, parents, and teachers. Encourage open discussions and invite guest speakers, policymakers, and education experts to share their insights.

By actively involving your community, you can create a collective movement for change.

Advocacy is a crucial aspect of active citizenship. Use various channels to communicate your ideas and concerns to policymakers. Write letters, emails, or petitions to your local representatives, education boards, and government officials. Attend public hearings and meetings to voice your opinions directly. Additionally, harness the power of social media to raise awareness, share your experiences, and build support for your cause.

Remember that change takes time and perseverance. Building a culture of active citizenship requires continuous effort and dedication. Stay committed to your goals and celebrate small victories along the way. Collaborate with other student organizations, schools, and institutions to create a broader impact. By actively participating in the policy-making process, you can shape the future of education and ensure that your voice is heard.

In conclusion, fostering a culture of active citizenship among students is essential to influencing education policy. By becoming informed, taking action, engaging the community, and advocating for change, you have the power to create a positive impact on education policies that directly affect you and your peers. Embrace your role as active citizens, and together, let us shape a brighter future for education.

Chapter 7: Overcoming Barriers to Student Participation

Addressing Ageism and Stereotypes in Education Policy Discussions

In recent years, there has been a growing recognition of the need to include student voices in education policy discussions. Students are the primary stakeholders in the education system, and their insights and experiences are invaluable in shaping policies that directly impact their lives. However, one aspect that often goes unnoticed in these discussions is the presence of ageism and stereotypes.

Ageism refers to the discrimination or prejudice against individuals based on their age. In education policy discussions, ageism can manifest in various ways, such as dismissing the opinions of younger students due to assumed inexperience or undermining the perspectives of older students due to perceived irrelevance. These stereotypes not only hinder the inclusion of diverse voices but also inhibit the development of comprehensive and effective policies.

It is crucial for students to recognize and challenge ageism and stereotypes in education policy discussions. By doing so, we can ensure that policies are inclusive, equitable, and representative of the diverse needs and realities of students across all age groups.

One way to address ageism is by actively involving students of different ages in policy-making processes. Younger students should be given opportunities to voice their concerns and ideas, as their fresh perspectives can offer unique insights into the challenges they face in the education system. Similarly, older students should not be overlooked or dismissed; their experiences can provide valuable guidance and wisdom in shaping policies that cater to the needs of students at various stages of their academic journey.

Another crucial step is to challenge stereotypes associated with age. It is essential to recognize that age does not determine the validity or relevance of one's opinions. Each student, regardless of their age, brings a valuable perspective to the table. By encouraging open dialogue and actively listening to each other's viewpoints, we can break down these stereotypes and create an inclusive environment for all students.

Furthermore, education policymakers and stakeholders must actively seek out and consider the diverse voices of students. This includes students from different backgrounds, ethnicities, abilities, and socioeconomic statuses. By incorporating a wide range of student experiences, policies can be designed to address the specific needs and challenges faced by different student groups.

In conclusion, addressing ageism and stereotypes in education policy discussions is crucial for fostering an inclusive and effective decision-making process. By recognizing the value of student voices across all age groups and challenging assumptions based on age, we can create policies that truly reflect the needs and realities of students. As students, it is our responsibility to advocate for the inclusion of diverse voices in these discussions, ensuring that policies are equitable and serve the interests of all students.

Navigating Power Structures and Hierarchies in Education Institutions

In today's educational landscape, it is crucial for students to understand and navigate power structures and hierarchies within education institutions. As students, you have a unique perspective and voice that can greatly influence education policy. This subchapter aims to empower you with the knowledge and strategies to effectively navigate these power dynamics and bring about positive change.

Firstly, it is essential to gain an understanding of the existing power structures within your educational institution. Recognize the roles and responsibilities of various stakeholders such as teachers, administrators, and policymakers. Identify the decision-making processes and channels of communication. This knowledge will enable you to identify where your voice can have the most impact.

Once you have a grasp of the power structures, it is important to develop effective advocacy skills. Understand that your voice matters and that you have the power to influence education policy. Educate yourself on the issues that concern you and the broader public policy landscape. Stay informed about current debates and research in education. This will provide you with the evidence and knowledge needed to support your arguments and proposals.

Building relationships is another crucial aspect of navigating power structures. Establish connections with teachers, administrators, and policymakers who share your passion for improving education. Attend school board meetings, join student councils, or participate in policy forums to engage in dialogue with decision-makers. By forming alliances and networks, you can amplify your voice and increase the likelihood of your ideas being heard.

However, it is important to recognize that power structures can be resistant to change. Be prepared for potential pushback or indifference. Do not be discouraged by initial setbacks. Persistence is key. Utilize various advocacy strategies, such as writing letters to policymakers, organizing student-led initiatives, or utilizing social media platforms to raise awareness and garner support. Remember, your voice has the power to create positive change.

Lastly, it is crucial to collaborate with other student advocates and organizations. Join forces with like-minded individuals who are also passionate about education policy. By working together, you can pool resources, share knowledge, and amplify your collective impact. Collaboration also provides a platform for diverse voices to be heard, ensuring that policies and decisions are inclusive and equitable.

In conclusion, navigating power structures and hierarchies within education institutions is essential for students who wish to influence education policy. By understanding the existing power dynamics, developing advocacy skills, building relationships, persisting in the face of adversity, and collaborating with others, you can effectively navigate these structures and bring about positive change in the realm of education policy. Your voice matters, and it has the power to shape the future of education for generations to come.

Resolving Conflicts and Building Consensus among Diverse Student Groups

In an increasingly diverse society, conflicts and disagreements are bound to arise. This is especially true within educational settings, where students from various backgrounds and perspectives come together to learn and engage. However, the ability to resolve conflicts and build consensus among diverse student groups is essential not only for maintaining a peaceful and inclusive environment but also for influencing education policy effectively.

The first step to resolving conflicts is to foster open and respectful communication. Encouraging students to express their opinions and concerns freely, while listening attentively to others, can help create an atmosphere of understanding and empathy. It is important to remember that each student's voice is valuable and that their experiences shape their perspectives. By actively listening to one another, students can gain a deeper understanding of different viewpoints and work towards finding common ground.

Building consensus requires collaboration and compromise. It is crucial to establish shared goals that reflect the needs and aspirations of all students involved. By identifying common interests and values, students can find ways to work together towards a mutually beneficial solution. This process may involve brainstorming, negotiation, and seeking alternative perspectives. Emphasizing the importance of teamwork and encouraging students to understand the value of compromise can lead to more effective and inclusive decision-making.

In order to effectively influence education policy, students must also learn to engage with public policy processes. This includes understanding how policies are developed, who the key decision-makers are, and how to effectively advocate for change. By participating in public hearings, writing letters or petitions, and engaging with local and national policymakers, students can ensure that their voices are heard and their concerns are taken into account. Additionally, forming alliances with like-minded organizations and individuals can amplify their collective impact.

Resolving conflicts and building consensus among diverse student groups is not always easy, but it is a crucial skill to develop. By promoting open dialogue, encouraging collaboration, and empowering students to engage with public policy, we can create a more inclusive and equitable education system. The power of student voices lies in their ability to foster change and influence policy decisions that impact their lives. Together, we can shape the future of education and ensure that every student's voice is heard and valued.

Chapter 8: The Future of Student Voices in Education Policy

Innovations in Education Policy Advocacy

Education policy plays a crucial role in shaping the future of students and the overall quality of education. It is a framework that outlines the guidelines, regulations, and strategies necessary for the effective functioning of educational systems. However, in order for these policies to truly be effective, they must take into account the voices and perspectives of the very individuals they are designed to benefit - the students themselves. This chapter explores the power of student voices in influencing education policy and highlights some innovative approaches to education policy advocacy.

In recent years, there has been a growing recognition of the importance of student involvement in policy decisions. Students are the primary stakeholders in education, and their unique perspectives and experiences can provide valuable insights into the effectiveness of existing policies and potential areas for improvement. By actively engaging students in the policy-making process, policymakers can ensure that their decisions align with the actual needs and desires of the student community.

One innovative approach to education policy advocacy is the use of technology. With the ever-increasing presence of digital platforms and social media, students now have more opportunities than ever to voice their opinions and concerns. Online platforms enable students to connect with one another, share their experiences, and collectively advocate for change. Social media campaigns, online petitions, and virtual town halls are just a few examples of how students are leveraging technology to amplify their voices and effect change in education policy.

Another innovative approach is the establishment of student-led organizations and advocacy groups. These groups empower students to come together, organize, and advocate for their interests at both the local and national levels. By providing a platform for students to articulate their perspectives, these organizations ensure that student voices are not only heard but also taken seriously by policymakers. Furthermore, they foster leadership skills and civic engagement among students, empowering them to actively participate in shaping their own educational experiences.

Lastly, innovative education policy advocacy involves fostering partnerships between students and policymakers. By creating opportunities for dialogue and collaboration, policymakers can gain a deeper understanding of the challenges students face and the changes they desire. This collaboration can lead to more effective policy decisions that reflect the realities of students' lives and aspirations.

In conclusion, the power of student voices in influencing education policy cannot be underestimated. By actively involving students in the policy-making process, leveraging technology, establishing student-led organizations, and fostering partnerships, policymakers can ensure that education policies are responsive, relevant, and truly beneficial to the student community. Students are the driving force behind educational change, and their voices must be heard and valued in the pursuit of a better and more equitable education system.

Predicting Trends and Opportunities for Student Voice Movements

In recent years, there has been a growing recognition of the power of student voices in influencing education policy. Students are increasingly seen as important stakeholders in shaping their own educational experiences, and their perspectives and insights are invaluable in improving the quality of education systems. As students, you have a unique perspective on the challenges and opportunities within the education system, and it is essential to understand how to predict trends and identify opportunities for student voice movements.

One of the key trends that can be observed in the student voice movement is the increasing use of technology as a means of amplifying student voices. The advent of social media platforms and online forums has provided students with powerful tools to express their opinions and connect with like-minded individuals. By harnessing the potential of technology, students can reach a wider audience, mobilize support, and advocate for meaningful change in education policies.

Another trend to watch out for is the growing emphasis on diversity and inclusion within student voice movements. It is essential to recognize that students come from diverse backgrounds and have unique experiences and perspectives. By embracing diversity and ensuring that all voices are heard, student voice movements can become more inclusive and effective in advocating for policies that benefit all students, regardless of their socio-economic status, race, gender, or ability.

Furthermore, an emerging opportunity lies in the collaboration between students and policymakers. As the recognition of student voices increases, policymakers are becoming more receptive to engaging with students in decision-making processes. This presents an excellent opportunity for students to actively participate in shaping education policies and programs that directly impact their lives. By fostering partnerships and building bridges with policymakers, students can create a more student-centered and responsive education system.

To be effective in predicting trends and identifying opportunities, students interested in public policy must stay informed and engaged. Keeping a pulse on current events, attending education conferences, and actively participating in student organizations can provide valuable insights into the evolving landscape of student voice movements. Additionally, it is crucial to leverage social networks and online platforms to connect with other student advocates and stay updated on emerging trends and opportunities.

In conclusion, predicting trends and identifying opportunities for student voice movements is crucial for students interested in public policy. By staying informed, leveraging technology, embracing diversity, and fostering partnerships with policymakers, students can play a significant role in shaping education policies that reflect their needs and aspirations. The power of student voices should not be underestimated, and by actively engaging in the student voice movement, you can be a catalyst for positive change in education.

Inspiring the Next Generation of Student Advocates

As students, we possess a unique power to shape the future of education policy and create positive change in our communities. The journey towards becoming effective advocates may seem daunting, but with determination and a clear vision, we can make a significant impact on public policy. This subchapter aims to inspire and guide the next generation of student advocates, providing invaluable insights and strategies to amplify our voices and influence education policy for the better.

First and foremost, it is crucial to recognize the significance of our lived experiences. As students, we intimately understand the challenges and opportunities within our educational systems. Our voices are a powerful tool to shed light on pressing issues, advocate for improvements, and ensure that our perspectives are heard. By sharing our stories, we can humanize policy debates and make a compelling case for change.

To become effective advocates, we must educate ourselves on the intricacies of public policy. Understanding how policies are developed, implemented, and evaluated allows us to navigate the system more effectively. By staying informed about local, state, and national education policies, we can identify areas that require attention and develop targeted strategies for advocacy.

Collaboration is another key aspect of successful student advocacy. By joining forces with like-minded individuals, student organizations, and community partners, we can amplify our impact and advocate for change on a larger scale. Building relationships with policymakers, educators, and other stakeholders will also broaden our influence and provide valuable opportunities for dialogue and collaboration.

Technology has revolutionized advocacy efforts, providing us with powerful platforms to share our ideas and mobilize support. Utilizing social media, blogging, and video-sharing platforms allows us to reach a wider audience and engage with policymakers directly. By harnessing the power of technology, we can effectively communicate our messages, rally support, and inspire others to join our cause.

Finally, self-care and resilience are essential for sustaining our advocacy efforts. Advocacy work can be challenging and emotionally draining at times. Taking care of our well-being, seeking support from mentors and peers, and celebrating small victories will ensure that we can continue to make a difference in the long run.

In conclusion, as students passionate about public policy, we have the power to shape the future of education. By recognizing the importance of our voices, educating ourselves, collaborating with others, utilizing technology, and practicing self-care, we can inspire change and influence education policy for the better. Let us rise to the challenge, channel our passion, and become the next generation of student advocates who transform the educational landscape for generations to come.

Conclusion: Harnessing the Power of Student Voices for a Brighter Educational Future

As students, we may often feel like our voices are not heard or valued when it comes to shaping education policy. However, it is essential to recognize that our perspectives and experiences are invaluable in creating a brighter educational future. The power of student voices should never be underestimated, and it is crucial for us to harness this power and use it to influence education policy effectively.

Public policy plays a significant role in shaping the educational landscape. It determines the curriculum, teaching methods, funding, and overall direction of our educational institutions. As students, we are the ones directly impacted by these policies, so it is only natural that we have a say in shaping them. Our firsthand experiences provide valuable insights and perspectives that policymakers may lack.

In recent years, there has been a growing recognition of the importance of including student voices in the policy-making process. Many educational institutions and policymakers have started actively seeking out student input through various means, such as surveys, focus groups, and student-led organizations. This shift demonstrates a greater acknowledgment of the fact that we are the primary stakeholders in the education system.

By actively engaging with policymakers and advocating for our needs and concerns, we can influence the decisions that directly impact us. We must seize every opportunity to make our voices heard, whether it be through participating in town hall meetings, writing opinion pieces, or meeting with policymakers directly. Our collective voices can create a powerful impact and bring about positive change.

Furthermore, it is essential for us to collaborate with other stakeholders, such as teachers, parents, and administrators. By building strong partnerships and alliances, we can present a united front and amplify our messages. Together, we can advocate for equitable funding, inclusive curriculum, safe learning environments, and policies that prioritize student well-being and success.

In conclusion, the power of student voices is immense and should not be underestimated. We have a unique perspective and firsthand experiences that can contribute to shaping education policy. By actively engaging with policymakers, collaborating with other stakeholders, and advocating for our needs, we can create a brighter educational future for ourselves and future generations. Let us harness our power and work towards a more inclusive, equitable, and student-centered education system.

www.ingramcontent.com/pod-product-compliance
Lightning Source LLC
Chambersburg PA
CBHW050617160726
48003CB00003B/1227